Books in the Linkers series

Homes discovered through Art & Technology
Homes discovered through Geography
Homes discovered through History
Homes discovered through Science

Myself discovered through Art & Technology
Myself discovered through Geography
Myself discovered through History
Myself discovered through Science

Toys discovered through Art & Technology
Toys discovered through Geography
Toys discovered through History
Toys discovered through Science

Water discovered through Art & Technology
Water discovered through Geography
Water discovered through History
Water discovered through Science

Reprinted 2001
First paperback edition 1996
First published 1996 in hardback by A&C Black (Publishers) Limited
37 Soho Square, London W1D 3QZ

ISBN 0-7136-4572-5
A CIP catalogue record for this book is available from the British Library.

Some of the people featured in this book are models.
Commissioned photographs by Zul Mukhida
Artwork by John Yates
Design by Jean Wheeler

Acknowledgements

Beamish, The North of England Open Air Museum; 13, 17 (right), 20 (right), 21, Chapel Studios;
4 (right), 8, 10 (left), 16 (left), 20 (left), Positive Images; 4 (left), 10, 12 (right), 14, 15 (both), 19 (both),
23 (both), Topham; 17 (left), Tony Stone Images; 22, Zefa; 12 (left).

Printed and bound in Italy by L.E.G.O.

Myself

discovered through

History

Karen Bryant-Mole

Contents

A & C Black • London

Me

This is a photograph of a boy called Robert.

Robert is seven years old.
How old are you?

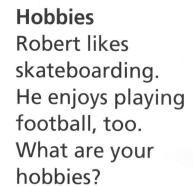

Hobbies
Robert likes skateboarding.
He enjoys playing football, too.
What are your hobbies?

Friends

Robert has a best friend, called Thomas.
What are your friends called?

The answers to these questions are all about yourself at this moment, or now.

'Now' is sometimes called 'the present'.

Days and weeks

Things that have already happened
have taken place 'in the past'.
You said your first word in the past.
Now you can say lots of words!

Yesterday
Kitty is eating toast for
breakfast.

Yesterday she ate cereal
for breakfast.
Yesterday is one day in
the past.
The time between one
breakfast and the next
is one whole day.

Last week

Kitty has a violin lesson on Tuesdays.

The time between lessons is one whole week.
Last week she was given a new piece to learn.
This week she can play it quite well.

Can you think of something that you did yesterday and something that you did last week?

Years

It's James' birthday.
He has a birthday present to open.
He still enjoys playing with the
walkie talkie he got for his
last birthday.

The time between birthdays
is one whole year.

Annual

This is a picture of a Christmas tree.
Christmas, like birthdays, only happens
once a year.
Another word for 'once a year' is 'annually'.
Can you think of any other special occasions
which happen annually?

Dates

Different years are called by different numbers.
This is a picture of James' dad when he was
a baby. He was born in 1966.
The year before he was born was called 1965.

The further back into the past you go, the
lower the number.
In which year were you born?

My family

Your family usually just means the people you live with.
But it can mean all your relatives, too.

Relatives
This photograph
was taken at a
wedding.

In the picture
there are aunts
and uncles,
mums and dads,
nephews
and nieces,
grandparents
and cousins.

Family tree

You can show how members of your family are related
to each other by drawing a family tree.

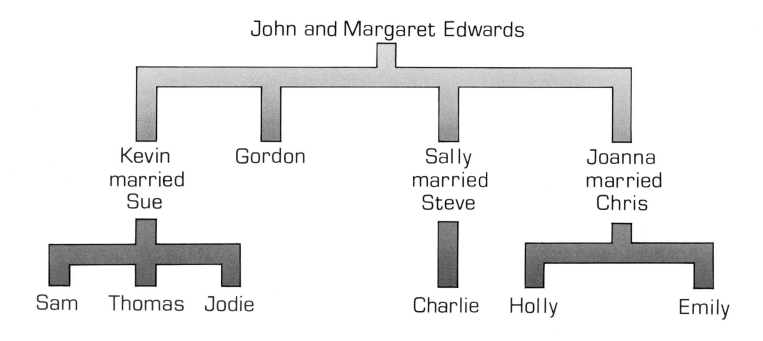

John and Margaret Edwards

Kevin married Sue   Gordon   Sally married Steve   Joanna married Chris

Sam   Thomas   Jodie   Charlie   Holly   Emily

Start with either your mum's parents or your dad's parents.
Then put in your mum or dad and their brothers and sisters.
If they got married, add in the names of the people
they married.
Finally, put in the names of any children they have.

In the past

There are lots of ways to find out about your family in the past.

Photographs
You could ask your parents and your grandparents whether they have any photographs of themselves when they were younger.

This picture was taken in 1958. In those days most photographs were in black and white.

Talking

You could talk to your relatives and ask them what life was like when they were children.

Artefacts

Your relatives may have kept things from their childhood, such as a favourite toy or a certificate from school. Objects from the past, like these, are sometimes called artefacts.

The following pages will give you some ideas of things to find out about your family in the past.

My clothes

Over the years, the type of clothes worn by you and your family have changed. So have the fabrics they are made from.

Acrylic
Charlie likes wearing tracksuits.

They feel soft and comfortable.

They are made from acrylic and are easy to wash in the washing machine.

Fashion
Charlie's dad's purple flared trousers were very fashionable at the time.

He's not quite sure why he was wearing his slippers in the garden!

Flannel

Charlie's grandpa wore grey, flannel shorts to school. Flannel is made from woven wool.

The girls usually wore cotton dresses.

Flannel and cotton are both made from natural materials.

My holidays

Today, people often travel much further from home than they used to in the past.

Greece

Kate and her family went to Greece last year.
The weather was hot and the sea was warm.
They flew to Greece in a plane and stayed in a hotel.

Britain

Kate's mum and auntie used to have a two week summer holiday in Britain.

They rented a cottage in a village near the sea and travelled there by car. Sometimes the sea was very cold.

Day trips

Kate's granny didn't go away for a long summer holiday.
Instead, she was taken on day trips to the seaside.
People often wore their ordinary clothes on the beach and tucked them up if they wanted to go for a paddle.

My home

Our homes and the things we have in them have changed a great deal over the years.

Electricity
William's home is full of electrical gadgets. A television, a video and a CD player can be seen in this picture.

How many things in your home are powered by electricity?

Heating

This is what William's dad's home looked like when he was a child.

The television only showed programmes in black and white. Low tables, called coffee tables, were very popular.

Coal

William's grandfather had a coal fire in his lounge.
As well as heating up the room, it also heated the water that came out of the hot taps.
There is a toasting fork hanging up next to the fire.

My toys

Children have always enjoyed playing with toys.

Jeep
Holly loves her pink jeep.
It is powered by a big battery.

She likes to ride it around the garden.

Pram

Holly's mum was given this pram for Christmas when she was two years old.
She had a special doll, called Susan, that she liked to push in the pram.

Trike

Holly's granny's favourite toy was her trike.
She used to ride it up and down the pavement outside her house.

Toys like these have been around for a long time.
But, over the years, the designs, the materials they are made from and the way they are powered have changed.

My school

The way you are taught at school is probably very different to the way your grandparents were taught.

Finding out
Luke likes working on the classroom computer.
He also likes working with the other children on his table to find out about things.

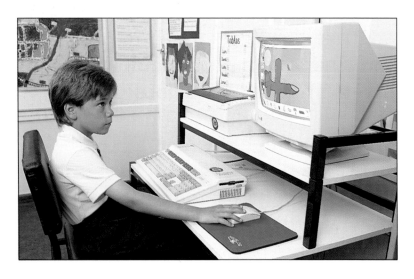

New school
Luke's dad went to a school that had just been built.
It was bright and airy, with lots of space.
Many children went to schools in much older buildings.

Blackboard
Luke's grandpa spent a lot of time copying work that the teacher wrote on the blackboard.
When the teacher wanted to show them something on the blackboard, she pointed at it with a stick.

My hobbies

After coming home from school, children spend their free time in lots of different ways.

Tennis
Rosie loves playing tennis.
In the summer she has tennis lessons.
Rosie also goes to gymnastics.
She does gymnastics all year round.

Ballet

Rosie's mum and auntie went to ballet lessons.
Their mum, Rosie's granny, took this picture of them practising in the garden.

Playing

When Rosie's granny was little, few children had lessons after school. She spent her free time playing with the children who lived next door.

Finding out about your family's past will help you to build up a picture of how life has changed over the years.

Glossary

acrylic a type of fabric, made in a factory

artefacts things that are made by people, usually from the past

certificate writing on paper or card that says what someone has done

designs plans to help you make something

fabrics the sort of materials used to make clothes and curtains

flared get wider

gadgets small machines

relatives people who belong to your family

toasting fork a long fork that could be used for toasting bread or crumpets by being held in front of an open fire

trike a three-wheeled cycle

Index

How to use this book

This book takes a familiar topic and focuses on one area of the curriculum: history. The book is intended as a starting point, illustrating one of the many different angles from which a topic can be studied.

It should act as a springboard for further investigation, activity or information seeking.

The following list of books may prove useful.

Further books to read

Series	Title	Author	Publisher
Changing Times	All Titles	Ruth Thomson	Watts
History Mysteries	All Titles	G. Tanner & T. Wood	A&C Black
History from Photographs	All Titles	K. Cox & P. Hughes	Wayland
Living in the ...	All Titles	R. Rees & J. Maguire	Heinemann
People through History	All Titles	K. Bryant-Mole	Wayland
Starting History	All Titles	Stewart Ross	Wayland
Talkabout Books	Then and Now	H. Amery	Usborne
Turn of the Century	All Titles	Various	A&C Black
Who Lived Here?	My Victorian Home	K. Bryant-Mole	Watts
	My 1930s Home	"	
	My 1950s Home	"	